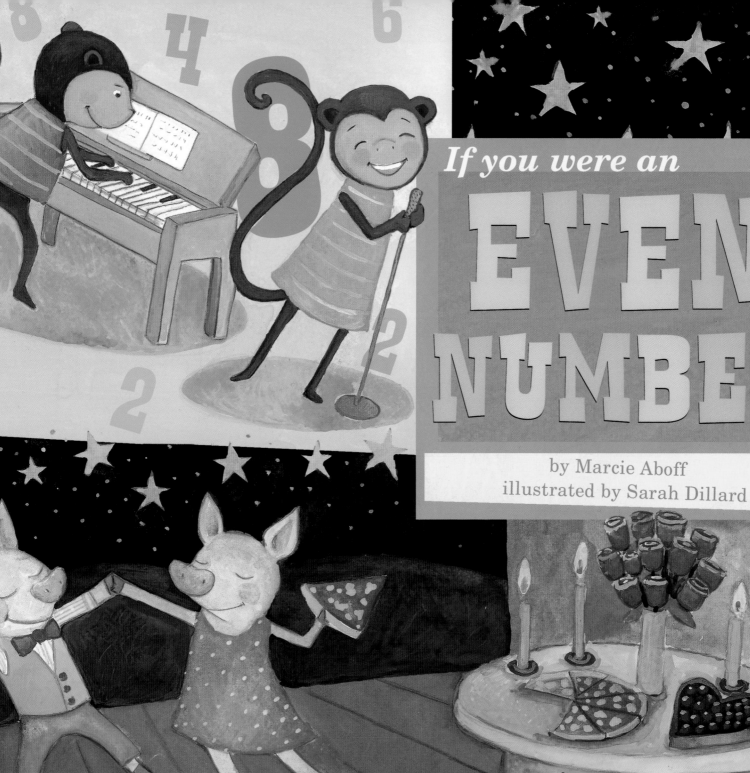

If you were an

EVEN
NUMBER

by Marcie Aboff

illustrated by Sarah Dillard

PICTURE WINDOW BOOKS
Minneapolis, Minnesota

even number—a number that is divisible by two

Editor: Christianne Jones
Designers: Nathan Gassman and Hilary Wacholz
Page Production: Melissa Kes
The illustrations in this book were created with acrylics.

Picture Window Books
151 Good Counsel Drive
P.O. Box 669
Mankato, MN 56002-0669
877-845-8392
www.picturewindowbooks.com

Printed in the United States of America.

All books published by Picture Window Books
are manufactured with paper containing at least
10 percent post-consumer waste.

Library of Congress Cataloging-in-Publication Data
Aboff, Marcie.
If you were an even number / by Marcie Aboff;
illustrated by Sarah Dillard.
p. cm. — (Math fun)
Includes index.
ISBN 978-1-4048-4796-5 (library binding)
ISBN 978-1-4048-4797-2 (paperback)
1. Numbers, Natural—Juvenile literature. I. Dillard,
Sarah, 1961- ill. II. Title.
QA141.3.A26 2009
513.2—dc22   2008006454

Special thanks to our advisers for their expertise:

Stuart Farm, M.Ed., Mathematics Lecturer
University of North Dakota

Terry Flaherty, Ph.D., Professor of English
Minnesota State University, Mankato

If you were an
even number...

3

... you could make a romantic meal for 2 with 4 candles, 8 pieces of pizza, 12 roses, and 24 pieces of chocolate.

If you were an even number, you would be divisible by 2. You would never have a remainder.

A group of 8 animals wanted to board the roller coaster. The ride had 4 cars.

The 2 mice took the first car.

The 2 birds took the second car.

The 2 bears took the third car.

The 2 cats took the fourth car.

The 8 animals were evenly divided into 4 cars.
Both 8 and 4 are even numbers.
No one got left out.

If you were an even number, your last digit would be 0, 2, 4, 6, or 8.

The leaping lizards played with 10 jacks.

The funny frogs played with 26 marbles.

The puzzled penguins played
with a deck of 52 cards.
Go fish!

If you were an even number, you would be between two odd numbers. You would be every other counting number on a number line, starting with 2.

Mrs. Rabbit asked the class to match the pictures on the board to the even numbers on the number line.

If you were an even number, you could add another even number to yourself. You would always get another even number.

The dog chased 2 balls.
Then he chased 4 more balls.
The dizzy dog chased 6 balls.

2+4=6

$$8 + 10 = 18$$

The cat climbed 8 branches.
Then he climbed 10 more branches.
The crazy cat climbed 18 branches.

If you were an even number, you could be an instrument and make beautiful music.

Marvin tapped 2 drumsticks.

Mary plucked 6 strings on a guitar.

Milt played 88 keys on a piano.
Melanie sang 8 sassy songs.

The 4 monkeys rocked the house!

If you were an even number, you could cheer at a football game.

"Say it loud—2, 4, 6, 8!
Who do we appreciate?"

"Even numbers, even numbers, yeah, even numbers!"

If you were an even number, you would stand on two feet, four feet, or eight feet. You wouldn't stand on one foot, because that's odd!

The 8-footed spider helped the 2-footed penguin and the 4-footed polar bear pack to go and visit their friend, the flamingo.

If you were an even number, you could go to a twins' picnic.

Two by 2, all of the animals came to the twins' picnic. Two pigs cooked 12 hot dogs, 10 hamburgers, and 22 ears of corn.

You would be 2 cool 4 words ...

... if you were an even number.

FUN WITH EVEN NUMBERS

Gather as many pennies as you can find and answer the questions below.

1. How many pennies did you collect in all? Is it an even number?

2. Count the pennies by twos. See how high you can count.
Are there any pennies left over?

3. Put all of the pennies in a cup. Toss the pennies on the floor.
How many pennies have heads showing? Is it an even number?
Now do the same thing counting tails.

4. See if you can stack the pennies without them falling over.
Count them as you stack them. How many pennies can you
stack before they fall over? Was it an even number?

Glossary

digit—a number between zero and nine

divisible—able to be separated into equal parts

even number—a number that is divisible by two

odd number—a number that is not divisible by two

remainder—a leftover number

To Learn More

More Books to Read

Chrismer, Melanie. *Odd and Even Socks.* New York: Children's Press, 2005.

Ekeland, Ivar. *The Cat in Numberland.* Chicago: Cricket Books, 2006.

Fisher, Doris, and Dani Sneed. *My Even Day.* Mount Pleasant, S.C.: Sylvan Dell Pub., 2007.

On the Web

FactHound offers a safe, fun way to find Web sites related to topics in this book. All of the sites on FactHound have been researched by our staff.

1. Visit *www.facthound.com*
2. Type in this special code: 1404847960
3. Click on the FETCH IT button.

Your trusty FactHound will fetch the best sites for you!

Index

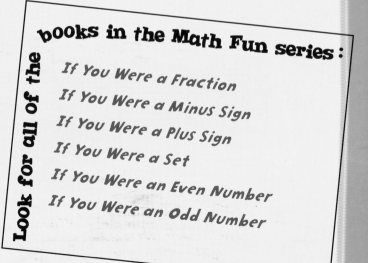

Look for all of the books in the Math Fun series:

If You Were a Fraction

If You Were a Minus Sign

If You Were a Plus Sign

If You Were a Set

If You Were an Even Number

If You Were an Odd Number